VIA Folios 187

Let It Be Extravagant

Published by Bordighera Press, an imprint of the John D. Calandra Italian American Institute of Queens College, The City University of New York.

25 West 43rd Street, 17th Floor, New York, NY 10036

All rights reserved. Parts of this book may be reprinted only by written permission from the publisher, and may not be reproduced for publication in media of any kind, except in quotations for the purposes of literary reviews.

Library of Congress Control Number: 2025942640

The photo featured on the cover was taken by the author.

© 2025, Michelle Reale

VIA Folios 187
ISBN 978-1-59954-242-3

LET IT BE EXTRAVAGANT

Michelle Reale

BORDIGHERA PRESS

For my parents

Has it ever struck you that life is all memory, except for the one present moment that goes by you so quick you hardly catch it going? —Tennessee Ford

Table of Contents

Misinterpreted	11
Catalytic	12
Volpe	13
At the Core	14
Auditory	15
Reliability	16
If You Should Find Yourself Voiceless	17
Moot	18
Somnolent	19
Somewhere They Worship Fruit	20
Canonical	21
Bellwether	22
Atavistic	23
Celestial Opportunities	24
Manifold	25
Superlatives	26
The Gate Through Which I Entered	27
The Things We Do And Have Always Done	28
Elemental	29
Inherited	30
Sanguination	31
Fever Dream	32
Mussolini's Balcony	33
The Old Country	34
My Father's X-ray	35
When Summer Begins To Die	36
Modigliani Knew Them All	37
Lupini Beans	38
Let It Be Extravagant	39
Wound	40
Curio	41
The Eternal City	42
Truncated	43
Suburban Neighborhood Pastoral	44
Spoiled	45

Attending Mass With My 90 Year Old Father	46
Chronotype	47
Manifold Illusions We Mistake For Happiness	48
Via Vecchia	49
Anointed	51
Somewhere In Calabria, 1952	52
At The Root	53
Portrait Of Great-Great Grandparents	54
Schematic	55
Sunday Sinatra	56
Pinned	57
Saccharine	58
Both Sides Now	59
My Mother Sings So That My Father Can Sleep	60
Emma Morano Died At 117 Years Of Age	61
Late Marriage	62
Dead Letter	63
A Single Surge	64
Against A Prescriptive Legacy	65
Corium, 1973	66
Foreshadowed	67
The Sleeping Beauty of Palermo	68
Insensate	69
Inherited	70
Umbra	71
Let Nothing You Dismay	72
All The Stars Are Shining	73
Acknowledgements	75
About the Author	77

If it's darkness we are having, let it be extravagant.
Jane Kenyon, "Taking Down the Tree"

Behold, here cometh the dreamer.
Let us slay him
And we shall see what will become of his dreams.
Genesis 37: 10-20

Like all dreamers, I mistook disenchantment for truth.
Jean Paul Sartre

MISINTERPRETED

In the cold light of day the bruised lips speak more than the bruised body might dare. Love generated by guilt will always exit through the unlocked door. We blame ourselves. There is a hollowed out space where we nest our young, but who are also urged to fly before anyone is ready for it to happen. The haunting sound of an airport piano played out of key but with sincerity gives a clue as to all that is wrong with this world. We adjust to the discordant with an ease like lying. What might sustain us in flight and during flights of fancy falls in and out of fashion. *Leaving is always inevitable.* The food we think we want still leaves us hungry and parched. We feed ourselves by hand, thinking it elemental, that it might make our ancestors smile. We imagine them, gapped toothed, teeth in the drawer only to be worn on a happy occasion. We are stripped down in what we want and what we can reasonably expect. Our spirits are like fish out of water. We divine a lineage of fulfillment without promises. *Like large sharks circling fresh blood.*

CATALYTIC

Swimming upstream is a talent. Movement abstracted from a particular situation is an exercise and not a particularly useful one. For instance, when I was born , a man leaned over me with a silver dollar on his chest. It gleamed with possibility, I was told. Intention counted for something then. His disappointment shone brighter than currency, which my mother tried to temper. She waved her hands as if shooing away a flock of featherless birds , which had nothing better to do than flap wildly with bird-like exclamations. My father dozed with his eyes at half-mast, a characteristic we'd become used to and for which he was known. The blood red Trillium along the border of the narrow house he'd cultivated for two generations was like a fortress. If he was lucky, there would be a third. Even precognitive, the smell of death wafted my way. *It would always be like this.* I could discern the timing of things. They called it a gift. The variables were always shifting, but I managed to find the right angle to things. That egress window was a portal to safety or it was nothing at all. Decorative was not in our nature. I would have given my life for the idle abstractions of my own family history, a way to do it properly, or just end it all together, but the story dictates we were always ever on our own. Assurances sucked noisily on a wayward breast. There is a ghostly foreshadowing linked forever to the knife that is sharp, but destined to rest in the linoleum lined drawer, no matter what it is capable of.

VOLPE

I wonder what she might have thought of my penchant for wishful thinking. My magical mindset where a situation could change simply because I willed it. I wonder what she would have thought of me hunched over the glow of my phone in the early a.m. , self soothing, eyes wild in the night, having slapped myself with an emotional gag order. How often I felt like St. Sebastien, with the sharp end of everyone's derision penetrating my many soft spots. How would she feel that I turned out to be the one who wears trauma like the coat she'd let me borrow– old, hooded and smelling of apprehension? It hung , dejected, on an ornate hook someone placed in that dark cellarway a century before, always at the ready. She grabbed that coat every time she hung clothes and remorse on the line, where they would freeze with indignation. What might she have to say now, the seer, who predicted her own death to the hour? I want future flowers for honest endeavors, but no one rewards that anymore. A voice that never quite hits an adequate pitch, might bring fortune, however wayward. My hands are open and my fingers are splayed. She could persuade me to stimulate my memories to influence my further moral decline. Or maybe she just affected the stony wall of so many silences that formed the backdrop of those formative years and beyond. There is cunning beyond what the spirit can imagine. Some might reject the mythology of the good omen, but not me. That screeching fox at the screen door had my attention. I imagine she watches dilemmas unfold from your unique vantage point in another dimension—watches the silken drops of someone's precious blood scatter like quicksilver, catching the light, spreading across the shy shrink and bold expansion of time.

AT THE CORE

Some traditions are like handmade heirlooms. We touch them with reverence, assuming their prominence in past lives. We note their rarified , theoretical breath, the last remnant of utility. We are all heart — pulsating, ruby pulp and veins like fragile vessels, carrying ancestral burdens through our bloodstreams. What is bred in the blood is memory. We want to stand in some perpetual light, to shine and subdivide. What's bred in the bone is longevity—all empty space to rearrange the flourishes we keep for special occasions. A heart preserved in the salt of the earth will contract. We are fortunate to still understand the laws of nature. A heart that expands from inactivity is paradoxical, but we appreciate fixed limits. It is the limitless nature of what the heart may be capable of that paralyzes us. This fact alone keeps our ancestors rolling in the fertile ground among the seedlings of bitter herbs, tearing at their fingernails with teeth that will grow and grow beyond the grave, feeding us for generation and generations to come.

AUDITORY

I place my ear at the mouth of a cleft in a rock. But I never understand a word when it is whispered to me. All rejection is circulatory, which means it runs right through you. My future son tells me one of his many dreams. This is how we communicate, as though underwater, sound muffled and aspirations delayed. He turns his eyes upward, given as he is to theatrics. He picks his teeth with the splintered bone of his ancestor I will name him after. He has access to all of those who have turned their backs on me, even in death. When he speaks, it is often in tongues, disembodied and without any real enunciation. My comfort is to go in search of the unforgotten. Many implore me with their rapidly moving eyes and their wringing hands. I suffer from chaos of the heart, all four chambers competing for equal attention. I cannot touch what I cannot see , but it never stopped me from trying. I am a casualty of geography. I have gone where my parents have dragged me in order to fulfill their dreams. I am the one who cannot prevent my father from folding the corners of every page of his Sunday Missal. I am the one who cannot silence the priest for just one moment so that I might discern cruelty and mayhem before they invite themselves to the threshold of my front door. I keep my wishes proximate, though I am a realist. I hum a melody of only two lines, but I am tone deaf. I am told the doors of heaven are open, but sometimes it all just feels too close. *Just too damn close.*

RELIABILITY

The crucifix on the pale wall will cast a shadow that dances. The fruit in the bowl will age with grace. The black thread and needle will find their rhythm. The pills in the old fashioned coffee saucer will find the right mouth. The foot in the shoe will clench like a claw. The mottled and misshapen eyes will twitch. The seer on the television will predict and we will blindly believe and follow. The old man two houses down will heave himself onto the ambulance gurney. He will not return. The fragile heads of flowers will droop dejectedly on their stems. The days will grow impatient and exhausted. The night will have us toss and turn with eyes wide open. Birds will fold themselves into their iridescent wings. Dinner will burn in the pot. Mothers with great anxiety will pace wooden floors with wailing infants while their partners will grind their teeth into dust. Piebald dogs and wolves bearing grudges will whine with resignation and loneliness. The evening news will drone yet paralyze us with fear. Spots will appear on the hand that trembles. The weather will have its way with us. We will verify unintelligible words for those who need it. We will stigmatize those within the domestic sphere appropriately. We will forget what it is we ever wanted to say. We will make room for what we no longer need but still want. We will peek over the high walls from the place we carelessly and begrudgingly call home.

IF YOU SHOULD FIND YOURSELF VOICELESS

There may be a grandmother somewhere who would be willing to carefully collect a drop or two of your tears and mix them with a sprig of rue and a lock of your hair. At this point you can forget all of the advantages that you possess. You could be the right person at the wrong time. We've all been there and we've cultivated the sorrowful look to prove it. If your small town is full of demons, narrow your field of vision and offer to polish their jackboots. The old *nonna* with the wild hair on her chin like a lightning rod sits demure and virgin-like by a lit stove keeping her secrets hidden beneath her sober apron. There is a cure for everything. *Say it.* If you can't interest your loved ones in collective memory, then who can you reasonably trust? Somewhere along the way the treachery of the alphabet came to haunt, but the throat betrayed itself. The superstition of angels can leave marks on the body. Their jealousy is unacknowledged, but present nonetheless. There is a bird with pooled blood in its eyes somewhere that sings all the songs you know by heart. *Just for you.*

MOOT

A woman isn't compost. And yet, she gets turned into the moss, the loamy earth receives her reluctantly with guilt. Beneath she lies stiff, her naked skull full of implications, but shining like onyx. It would be difficult not to discern a theme here. Insert a black diamond as a metaphor. What else can be said? There is a storehouse of bad intentions with guilty afterthoughts. With palms up a woman might bring bright flowers to your funeral and decorate your grave with legalese and understatement, but she would warn you first, even if she had to become a banshee to do so. Hucksters might hawk coarse cotton or satin for burial, but the dead don't feel a thing of this world. Wrap the extremities in something that might keep them dry for a while until they are forgotten, because we, after all, are fallible. Mold the lips to represent tolerance and long suffering. Wax and water will always be incompatible, a rare truth we can count on. Ritual makes us apprehensive, so instead we trade in the gestures of commerce, our true habitat. There are excuses enough to fill a casket of pure gold, but oh the price it would fetch. She might have been a gifted storyteller, a songbird yet to come into her own, but in so many instances, we can never really know for sure.

SOMNOLENT

When the fatigue began again, I welcomed it like an old friend, like the one who stopped calling right after we shared an expensive meal. After that, I told someone how I was tired right in my soul , which I felt was a feathery thing . I pointed to my sunken chest. They laughed but put great space between us. I hadn't meant for it to be funny. My emotions were leaking, like a valve that needed a tool to fix it, but that had not yet been invented. I hadn't meant to say it at all. I forgot how distance provides protection, though I was a threat to no one. Maybe they thought that their souls would feel tired, too. That I would transmit the wiggly germ of lethargy to their bright and bubbly nature. That ennui would strike them in their prime. I was so tired, and could sleep almost anywhere. *Go take a shower !* was a common refrain. But water sluicing over my body only made me think of the time before birth when I was submerged in a self-contained little world. How I must have floated in the superheated amniotic fluid, playing with my tiny toes and fingers. How each cigarette my mother smoked and with each inhalation, I got my own little boost. In my watery globe, my hair grew like tiny quills on my small head, evidence , they say, of my mother's heartburn. I've blocked the rest out. When my eyes droop, I tend to forget, despite all the evidence to the contrary, that , potentially, there are still places on earth where you don't have to sleep with one eye open.

SOMEWHERE THEY WORSHIP FRUIT

There were prickly pears everywhere. They nested in baskets and bowls were tucked into bureau drawers, in the glove compartments of cars, and hidden in clothes dryers. I knew of one woman, who could only speak on the Day of the Dead and had several rolled inside of her stained, terry cloth apron, right next to the paring knife that she needed for various purposes. There was nothing else to eat. Everyone loved the ruby fruit, except for me. I would have eaten anything—a cucumber with skin, an unshelled shrimp, a scrap of hard bread saved from the breakfast *zuppa*. A grandfatherly type came towards me in long strides I didn't think he was capable of. His eyes were protected against the sun by his fedora which sat high up on his head and his cigarette was persistent, glowing in his shaking, thick fingers. He was persuasive, but I had my mother's taurine nature. And I had a growling stomach to think about. He held out the prickly pear to me, and I sunk my teeth into the cactus-like flesh. I kept biting like an animal and spitting the skin on the ground. The smile drained from his face. Later, he would warn others about me, That I was impulsive and ungrateful. That I failed to abide by the local and time-tested ways. *Wasted a perfectly good goddamn piece of fruit*, he'd mumble, ambling up and down the sun soaked village. *O Dio,* the women would cry in response, peeling the fruit into bright colored bowls which they'd offer to the children who played in the courtyard, every day without fail, until dusk.

CANONICAL

The change from one season to another is a fissure in the brain. Even the grocery store flowers, sucking up the last of the slimy water from the thick rimmed vase are not immune to changes in the atmosphere, however minute. Throw open a window and pretend to be relatively unfettered. Reserve judgment for those who dress for the month and not the weather. The murmurations of starlings flying above snow in June, can have a tranquilizing effect if you listen to it for too long. Crack the egg and scramble the yoke with a fork, starting from the center outward, like you were taught to do. The implications of the dash of blood you see, are far reaching, but stay in the moment. We are reminded again and again that our ancestors were bred for brutality, for storm after storm, from battle to war. The shedding of blood, in certain circumstances, is nothing to be ashamed of. We are only afraid of what we might have to endure, somewhere out there alone, and without a coat to keep us warm when no one else will. Catch us unadorned, sloganeering on the outposts of funereal celebrations to which we were uninvited. Everyone wearing mourning clothes is not necessarily your friend. We are told we need ritual. A novena could summon cruelty, but that is a risk I can imagine taking. Life can be learned even if instructions are not followed to the letter. In certain countries they reserve praise for the rogue. In the end, there is an amulet for nearly everything.

BELLWETHER

The intuitive can sense when the spirit is low. The grinding thrum, a scourge and a threat to the more felicitous, those with the fortitude to see themselves through. How they sidestep, misstep, turn the deaf ear for fear of withering spirals that transport sound. We indulge ourselves in beliefs, console ourselves with fractured faith, diametrically opposed to our better instincts. We are febrile in our attempts to discern which of two hypotheses that fight each other might create the folklore that that we can build a foundation on. You can hear so many stories that you will start to believe anything. While the sea might give up its secrets reluctantly, we of flesh and bones are like martyrs willing to spill our life blood for transformation, for false intimacy, for entanglements we will convince ourselves we both need and want. The anterior cell of any feeling, particularly desire, is prone to fallibility. We live by threading the needle. We stare at the full moon. We light candles and watch the flames flicker until our eyes burn. When we peel the apple we let the spiral of skin fall to the ground. We let it brown, wrinkle and shrink, discerning what we can from it, leaving our objectivity outside, under the well-worn welcome mat. We know, *I mean we just know*, that whatever it is, it is not for us.

ATAVISTIC

Praise and envy have always existed on a continuum. I could never figure out the difference between an oppressor and a lover; the boot on the neck or a firm and loving hand on the shoulder is a conundrum I am still unraveling. I am no longer afraid of monastic tendencies. Secrets are always a bit shocking to the uninitiated , but can sow seeds that can grow into great revelations that arouse the curious among us. I have been looking my whole life for just the right mentor. So praise the exiles for their venerable sacrifices, and acknowledge their intrepid nature. Do not call them wanderers or nomads. Watch how initially they elicit sympathy with their downcast eyes, but later, because the threads of their collective coats refuse to properly unravel, disdain. They remain aloof because they have to be, but their eyes tell another story. *Read the glimmer in them.* They crossed boundaries that could only be imagined in the despot's mind, on heavy and reluctant feet. They traveled light save for their historical burdens and ambitious future plans. Sentence us all to death in absentia, but send your emissaries before us, just in case. Replace our dust-laden robes with white ones, with braided cords around our waists in the tradition of the saints we revere. We will read each other's thoughts in unison and raise our voices like we are participating in a grand opera devoid of an audience. In time let's all forget the places we came from and unfurl our gritty tongues to speak a new language , pulling our nostalgia for what was, up from the root. *They call this kinship.* A classical tragedy in all of its ancestral manifestations.

CELESTIAL OPPORTUNITIES

A star reaches the end of its life and , and in a luminous burst of light, a supernova is born. One can only imagine the pains it must take to birth one. The cosmic groans from the nether regions and sharp pain at the sparkling and pointed tips. The star weeping upon itself, keening for what is ending, fearful of power soon to be unleashed. When the dying star turns in on itself, things begin to happen. I want to think we are guided by that brilliant light, like a cosmic flashlight leading the way with our strong titanium arms helping to tug on the supernova , to spank it on its bottom, and welcome it to life. *We come from stars, but we are not stars, but maybe the difference is negligible.* We give ourselves up to that flash of light and let it swallow us whole. Light a candle and praise the obscure and forgotten saints. We will join them when the time is right.

MANIFOLD

I keep secrets folded away, just as I was taught. My sharp clavicle bulges with mutant tongues, dry, their heaving, babbling days now gone. They have fallen silent. This is profoundly evolutionary, and nothing for anyone to be afraid of. The mouth that no longer speaks has great value. The tongue that no longer wags becomes a precious relic. Our true natures have more durability than we would ever admit to. I gather what I can from those who don't know better, who were not instructed in the ways of social decorum. Before they know it, the delicious details of private lives have been scattered like seeds. *But isn't this our way?* In small villages, one word and then another determined survival. There are so many ways that this can be done. When one leans in close, remember to reward them with a word or two. Make them promise not to tell. My secrets shift from one place to another. I hold my own hands. I bring a cracked cup to my own lips. I sing myself to sleep under a vast array of conditions that cannot even be imagined. I talk to ghosts crouching in corners. I try to keep my talents from diminishing. My precipitous mourning has a genetic component. Still, the dead will accumulate into piles. The ancestors are never wrong. Somewhere, a voice calls out, mimicking all of my interior monologues. *I keep my own counsel.*

SUPERLATIVES

There is an old saying, but I will be damned if I can remember what it was. There are offshoots of rare plants that I would like to call by their scientific names, but nature itself abhors labels and so I adjust. Years have passed and I recall the scent of candles burning down to stumps in a damp church, the smell of wet funereal flowers that tickled my gag reflex. Your face, a mask of purity: untested, unbothered, unalive. I wanted to call everything God, but there are visionaries on every corner who have already staked their claim, and I am always late and unwelcome. Common decency dictates that I cede, go back to starching the altar cloths and spit polishing the monstrance. I give the priest a wake up call and drop an envelope with a paltry offering in the long-handled basket that passes in front of me. The difficulty of genuflection has a purpose—my mother advises me to offer up the pain for world peace, but as we speak, at least thirteen countries are either burning their own people or going after yours and my knees feel like individual pits of molten lava. Those who bear arms also plant flags in the loamy blood soaked earth and put words into the mouths of their citizenry. *Sing praise! Change your meandering course!* Respective efforts deserve recognition. I can be a strega in a month of Sundays. *Ring your bell and call it a day.*

THE GATE THROUGH WHICH I ENTERED

My father stared at me wordlessly for hours, while I twisted myself, small and nearly insignificant into life. A harbinger of my future existence. The air we breathed was stunted with loss. My mother, in between feedings, smoked cigarettes while she scrubbed and waxed floor boards. Her skin crackled and oozed. In the black and white photos with scalloped edges, of which there are few, I am wide-eyed and unsmiling, propped up by someone or something unseen. How I drifted in and out of both will and consciousness, not unlike the dying, and the inauspiciousness of my arrival would haunt me. If I was encouraged, it was toward a future that those with a wandering eye always ridiculously aspired to. I would be welcomed with garish smiles , the proffered hand, the church incense that could sting the eyes and transport to faraway lands with just a whiff. What I knew was that the stultified emotions of the long undiagnosed could lock one away. A first memory of awareness: a decorative plate hung on the kitchen wall with my parents' wedding date in curly script , a painted old time likeness of them both. My small hand to my face, my blue eyes blink wide with recognition. My parents, my emotional inheritance and no strangers to the unspoken, reposed in far corners of the house, entertaining assumptions and predictions. A fly silently flew with agitation around the room, grimly without an exit strategy. In time I would become numbed and habituated to a silence that I would never get used to.

THE THINGS WE DO AND HAVE ALWAYS DONE

Even good people will tell a story of a woman who leaves home to go and follow a man to God only knows where. The story circulates , a simplistic version at first adding layers as it goes along. Somewhere a hunter's eye is caught by a fraying ribbon around a thick trunk of a tree, surrounded by overgrowth. There are grown children who stare into fogged mirrors discerning facial omissions, differences. But haven't we always been this way, tender and awake, truly homesick every day of our lives'? Our nomadic mothers notwithstanding, it is worse not to be able to locate yourself in time. Every once in a while , we will go astray and leave ourselves, or someone will leave us where they found us: untamed and subversive. We are gifted storytellers, who cannot bear to keep our words to ourselves. The woman who left her home lives in the anterior cell of all fallibility, and she no longer looks like herself. After her husband passes through his rebellious stage, he will settle into old age with the ghostly ghazals he hears on dark nights with a full moon. On one fateful night he pressed her shoulder blades into sheetrock, and stigmata was born. We will tell what we know, and if we have to , we will improvise. The eyes that see us darkly will deem us decent, tongues like silver forks ready to strike.

ELEMENTAL

On the avenue, ghost signs blush on repurposed brick buildings. People are leaving us. It was bound to happen. Nothing can anchor them here anymore, not their cigarettes, mortgages, love affairs, imminent deadlines , unsaid proclamations of love, or their freshly stocked pantries. There are hollow spaces where they used to be, that we scream into, silk dopamine threads of being, left behind. Molecules of their breath hang in spaces that have outlived them, and will outlive us. Decay is marked by successive decades. Silk dopamine threads of being, left behind. Molecules of their dank breath hang in spaces that have outlived them, and will outlive us. The satin lined coffins are an aura that haunts our days. They leave their imprints like shadows on an X-ray. I see them, but I walk through them, too. They fidget in their somber clothes that were chosen for them. They pass on the fear of what they have endured and because we are porous in our grief, we understand and receive their inheritance. There are phases to everything and if we look close enough we can see the ending in every beginning. The new moon is elemental. Our desires continue to beg for care and the attention that we are too distracted to give ourselves. Time plays itself then is gone without even a glance in our direction.

INHERITED

While we crept balletic on our growing toes, silent in the gloaming, our mother's slept. Sisters, in proximate locations, eyes ringed with the fatigue of most women of the time from cigarettes, coffee, exhaustion, changing expectations and the length of the hem. I sang lullabies to the African violets that my aunt cultivated under artificial light in the dark basement, my hands and arms bathed in a purple hue I swore I could taste. My cousin counted the stitches in my mother's colonial afghan stuffed in a Wanamaker's bag, the colors burnt orange and chocolate brown that were all the rage. It would remain stubbornly unfinished. Hours sneaked upon us in soft- as- silk slippers, as the after school hours always slipped into early evening and curled around the dinner we never wanted. I was a clock watcher. My cousin tapped her newly acquired Timex. The world passed by with the sweep of the second hand. I felt hunger like a place I once loved but was destined never to return to. She always brushed her glossy hair in 100 strokes at one hour intervals. Our mother's hummed the chaotic music of perpetual fatigue. I remained in my school uniform for hours each night. The soft chair called to me. My cousin would phone and ask "anything yet?" I watched my mother sleep, mouth open, oblivious. *No, But if anything changes, I'll let you know.* My eyes were heavy as sandbags. I heard nothing but a cavernous yawn at uneven , though predictable intervals.

SANGUINATION

Before I learned how to torture a single metaphor into a poem, and waited out the hot rain on interminable summer nights, the blood flowed without restraint. I cataloged variations between myself and my father, who was the original bleeder, handkerchief forever to his face. It wasn't in him to betray a sorrowful emotion, though his nose did it for him, a crooked river of blood as consolation. My nosebleeds began as a pseudo couvade syndrome, and always occurred while I was in school, where the loss of blood corresponded nicely with the measuring of all of my many deficiencies. It was an education enough just to count how many things there were to lose. My father's blood spoke an in-between language to the memories that he couldn't. Mine spoke what was to be. That was the year that the old nun who sat in the office at the end of the hallway would usher me into the bathroom, push my face down and let the blood fall into shapes I could divine in the porcelain sink. She held a brass ring of keys to the back of my neck while I cried with great energy. When the bleeding slowed down, but did not stop, I was sent back to class. Later, I would cancel out passages in my diary to subvert my own loneliness. My father, wordlessly as was his way, offered a brand of sympathy I was unaccustomed to, like a church sermon gone rogue. Like a single metaphor writ large.

FEVER DREAM

Haste is not a virtue. What I would have sworn were memories, I now realize might have been dreams, tucked into the nautilus of a fevered brain cowering in a corner. *I have been so rash my entire life.* Slow living is extolled among the aged, but what else are they supposed to do? The dry mouths, gaping, and the rheumy eyes searching have seen better days. If I stretch the skin, like cellophane, across the cheekbones of my father's face, he becomes a blur, a thing out of focus , but the clock is still ticking and we count every one. My mother will crochet her own variegated shroud to save anyone else the trouble. Her grimace masquerades as a smile, and much pain is to be given up for the sanctity of the world. The humoral issues at play have fangs, and they are planted firmly in our necks. Our moon faces are waxy and tinged with yellow. They lack the grace we believe might save us. The breviary with its colorful ribbons collects dust on the nightstand, its pages warped, but still, it moans in the dark. Everything is beyond the urgent grasp. The shivering in the night, the drenching of sweat in the day is not an omen. *But it might as well be.*

MUSSOLINI'S BALCONY

It is good to trust others, but not to do so is much better.
—Benito Mussolini

In Rome I felt a fever. I navigated the uneven surface of the cobblestones. People milled about in desultory ways in the summer heat. A young mother gripped the hand of her son and yanked him to attention. *Walk* she commanded, as he rubbed his eyes, the delicate skin beneath them a study in violet. All around me I felt a great energy like my heart was lit from the inside by neon, knowing it could end at any moment. Mussolini's balcony, above, was unimposing though I realized the importance of symbols. I wondered how his frenzied supporters were able to discern their humble dreams from his rabid tyranny. The national flag swayed to and fro, as I lost perspective. A tired looking man with a beautiful wife stood still, her Fendi bag clutched to the delicate scaffolding of her chest aware of her own allure. I smelled the strong perfume and cigarette smoke that permeated everything. Somewhere, somehow, Mussolini hovered like an inconvenient memory. The banality of the scene caught me off guard. I was sweating profusely, perhaps on the verge of serious hallucination or heartbreak–I'd often had difficulty discerning one from the other. I needed something ice cold as an antidote. A small girl with narrow blue eyes stood watching a man with a milk snake wrapped around his thick wrist, a small jar for coins at his twisted feet. The balcony loomed like an imperative. I needed political and emotional orthodoxies that I could rely on or reject at the drop of a hat. *A crooked path that might lead me astray, but one that I might survive, nevertheless.*

THE OLD COUNTRY

The difference between a sarcophagus and an altar is pure intention. The dip and sway of grief can be prismatic in its display. There were good people for whom dying was not an option and tried to make the best of it. The old man who combed his hair in the mirror one morning and was found later that evening laying on the cold tile on the bathroom floor might have called himself lucky. The old women, in remembrance, wore clothing so black , they blocked out the sun. Tradition is a twisted foot wedged in the door of unbecoming. Strong coffee poured into miniscule cups can keep sorrow at bay for only so long. Oh, but the bitter, bitter taste it leaves on the parched and ridged tongue. We drink and pray to a negligent God for his distorted mercy in any way he'd like to send it.

MY FATHER'S X-RAY

reveals the spirit of *sprezzatura*. *This is his birthright.* His bones twisted in the clumsy ballet they are prone to when they make acquaintance with concrete. Feet aloft one moment, splayed the next. My father thinks wellness is nothing but tedium, so he mixes it up a bit just to keep us on our toes. We note this carefully. The X-ray did not reveal his sacred and studded heart, his brutal neutrality in most situations, but we asked the doctor, who seems to be aging himself, beyond what seems reasonable, to look anyway. He likes my father's stoicism, which has nothing to do with anything. He winks and tells him that he knows some women he's personally sent on to the afterlife who would like to meet a man who smiles through pain with stoicism. *An attractive trait,* the doctor adds as dust falls from his furry ears, a glint in his eye revealing his knowledge of what awaits him, too. Nevertheless, my father's X-ray, fluorescent and hanging on the wall, reveals all that it is capable of, the crack and crumble of time. But the aged vodka on the doctor's shelf is not medicinal, and he himself is no apothecary. *At least that much is evident.*

WHEN SUMMER BEGINS TO DIE

my mother begins to hear old time ballads, a deep voice crooning the vagaries of love and longing, on planets far away. It is difficult to pinpoint when it began. She enjoys the music immensely, but it interrupts her *telenovelas*. She says that the singing stops and starts in fits, and the man singing just might have a temper. Her unusually large ear, fit with a flesh colored hearing aid, twitches and swivels in different directions, doing reconnaissance, trying to pick up an errant musical signal. Her own mother, long gone, interrupts the musical broadcast with advice on being old, and how, at some point, your life is just full of generalizations and unanswered prayers. My mother tells her, *times have changed. English poets wrote sonnets for 400 years, now what?* But her mother recedes to a place some dream about, and the crooning begins again. My mother closes her eyes and smiles, saying *can you hear it?* I close the window before the novel cool air we desperately thought we wanted reaches her, like most things, unaware and unprepared.

MODIGLIANI KNEW THEM ALL

After *"Portrait of a Polish Woman,"* by Amedeo Modigliani

I recognized the dolorous length of the face. The tilt of the delicate head as if in confusion or doubt, the skin hued in jaundice. The hands placed demurely, though restlessly on the thigh bones. The thighs are covered in the coarse fabric of the sensible or the poor. The mouth is small with a confusion of muscles animating the appearance of misgiving, sadness. The jet black hair like a raven before flight. I recognized my foremother, in fact, all of my foremothers in her eyes. Modigliani knew them all, by each feature their passions, terrors, regrets and insincerities. With his brush he fashioned a woman from paint who speaks to me across generations and time. A woman who he would immortalize on canvas, to be venerated and adored, though she be created in ambiguity, and forever without a name.

LUPINI BEANS

I brought the cold jar into my room, a place of sad dolls, broken pencils and magic hats. I sat on the floor surrounded by the cold energy of the inanimate. My face was scrubbed clean, but the dirt under my fingernails was a remnant of my childish quest for treasures, wherever I might find them. Alone, I could hear nothing but my own ragged breath, puffing. I pushed my hand into the jar and scooped out two lupini beans, yellow, hard and briny. I worked their skins off with my tongue. The salt made me thirsty. I didn't stop chewing until they were mush, and small hard pieces were stuck in my teeth. My lips became white ,and my mouth puckered. The stomach ache came as I knew it would, like an old friend holding a grudge, the one my mother warned me about all the time. I laid on my side and fingered the green and yellow shag carpet while I watched one lone bean left, floating in the jar , like a child doing the dead man's float at a fancy swim club in a crowded pool, at high noon.

LET IT BE EXTRAVAGANT

There were no omens to speak of. Things either happened or they didn't. The bags of salt nailed into every doorway ensured that the evil spirits would have to count every grain before they entered, but shortcuts were taken, we know that now. We could feel them sidled up beside us when we were happiest, amorphous figures in black, undefined, and terrifying. We counted our blessings just in case, but knew that a phone call would come, sooner or later. My grandmother once looked across the street to see three of her many siblings, dead 50 years or more, gathered on the corner. One was smoking an unfiltered cigarette. *We believed every word.* As my mother made a cup of coffee one early evening, she saw her daughter-in-law's hand, dead from the cancer that ravaged her, lifted up to the outline of her unsmiling face, as though to say something, but thinking better of it. Later she described it as *a beautiful hesitation.* I called my mother the same evening to say that I, too, had seen her as she took the steps in my house two at a time until she reached the top. For years there was a room whose threshold I could not cross. People have grown weary listening to the nakedness of our dreams and visions. I have compassion for them, but only to a point. I hear a persistent hymn sung by a woman in a contralto voice that quivers, though I cannot discern the words, nor the direction from which it comes. Sorrow is always at the same distance from every center, extravagant and unashamed. I keep a window open in every room, a knife in every drawer.

WOUND

In the land of strong perfume and cigarettes, St. Sebastian's sacrifice has all but been forgotten. Martyrdom, though it still happens in suburban homes and on the battlefield, is out of fashion. Only the grimace and spiritual ineptitude of pain remains. Under the baking sun we force narratives of well-being, carefree, almost lyrical earnestness in the day to day trance we engage in. Distension of facial muscles could be an Art all its own, but no one would ever call it that and it would fetch precious little in the market. The main ingredient will always be potential, but we still need a rubric for it. We remain spectators among the masses of those with a grim turn to the mouth. We are vertical soldiers in the army of the humble. *Venerate or be venerated* sounds like a threat only if you have something to hide. When the arrow hits its mark it recognizes its beauty within this dimensional universe. Let the muscles seize, let the voice carry like a soloist at the juncture of sentimentality and salvation. *We all have our crosses to bear* remains a trite thing to say, but I've seen it manifested. If yours is heavily scented and teetering in limited edition shoes on ancient cobblestones you will do what you can to avoid it, or just pawn it off on someone less fortunate. There are those who get paid to suffer. I would tell you though, to go on the offensive. Draw your sword like a trained mercenary who just can't lose, and lay your 18k gold chances on the crooked line.

CURIO

There are houses built from genuine sorrow. Lock the doors and preserve what is best not shared. Distortions so profound as to alter time and space have been documented somewhere. There used to be a treatment for this. Nodes attached to the scalp, worn leather straps holding in place the body that might convulse , eyes flouting a gaze that could not follow anything. Forget birds pontificating in Greek or a single file of bright red lobsters nipping at your heels. The miserable have better things to do. Shellac me in the dusty truth. Inside a snow globe everything looks muted, though well-kept, and so pristine, that the only thing that could disturb the scene would be a lover's complaint that you might not even take seriously. Urban apathy and flying backwards are fatalistic tendencies, but aren't we all just trying to do our best? The finger pointing will never cease. The man with the wires attached to his head is like an ersatz Caesar banished to certain exile. His dusty possessions are tucked away where someday we might look at them from behind glass and wonder at the spectra of what passes for normal on any given day.

THE ETERNAL CITY

We are built to extend ourselves, but the shod feet taking one step after another on ancient stones, leading to a monument on a hill, has the potential to turn to sooty ash. It is folly to move too far from the decorative city fountains where you might plunge your head, or dip your breasts into its coolness, even though the locals will laugh at you, but really, not for long. They, too, are incinerated from the inside out. They too, now sport the ridiculous straw hats and visors that are customarily de *rigueur* of the pale, overweight tourists with their irritations and idiosyncrasies, who like to tell, with pride, how they have *no tolerance for the sun*. In cafes, people rest their heavy, sweaty heads on cool Formica tables while tired ceiling fans do endless dusty revolutions with barely a hint of relief. The *solleone* is pervasive, so forget the shade, the afternoon pasta, that sweating glass of wine that will have you staggering home, with your tongue arriving on the doorstep before you do. Devise a plan to be able to survive the heightened intensity of mercury, wherever you may find yourself. It's time to dream a different kind of dream now. Dig a hole and crouch in the arms of cool Mother Earth, before she breaks all the records then spins off, trailing sparks, to a faraway place, and turns her back on us forever.

TRUNCATED

Here is a story I always try to tell, but it never comes out right. My feelings are a stutter wearing jackboots, sputtering, all false starts with astonishing bravado. What I saw was sad tulips drooping on the kitchen windowsill in the lazy way that certain men love their children—well meaning affection, but devoid of action. Somewhere, but not here, I felt my way through dim light and discerned a forlorn looking woman wearing a diadem. She extended her arm to me, but never knowing what is good for me, I refused. Pointed stars pierced her and she bled silver rivulets of blood. What I thought was a premonition was just a desire to be reassured that I was loved. *Somebody, just listen, please.* I willed it with all my might, but I am told that nobody likes an emotional prompt. I breathed the thick air around me, and drew the iridescent moths who followed me here in single file, into my orbit. In the absence of light, I was a beacon, all shiny and lit from within. *Or rather I had the potential to be.* Houses stood like silent witnesses to irregular architecture, a victim of the sinister nature of time, and tastes that are forever changing. *How to say this?* Things eventually collapse. I was caught in the kind of void that longing after great pain creates. I wanted to fill the space with cosmic rays and energy fields that could penetrate the imagined world and animate those of us stuck in its vicious stupor. But please let me tell you, let me say it like this: *I had a golden hammer in my hand, but my God, if only I knew how to use it.*

SUBURBAN NEIGHBORHOOD PASTORAL

The gray squirrel under the bald tire. The faded beach towels over the front porch railing. Little girls with dirty hair and flip flops. The buzz and drone of a lawnmower. The small plastic pool on the front lawn. The red with white polka dotted lantern fly nymphs clustered on a Walnut tree. The faux cheerful, though sinister electronic tune of the ice cream man, inching his truck down the street. The dry dirt being blown around by an intermittent breeze. Dark clouds mixed with sun. A man with a glistening torso and hiking boots, his t-shirt wrapped around his head, shovel in hand. The mailman with a large, sweating bottle of water. The shades that are drawn against the relentless sun, like closed eyes. The reverberating sound of the basketball hitting the rim on the court over and over. The young mother with puffy eyes and a stringy ponytail doing a slow promenade up and down the street, menthol cigarette smoldering in her right hand. The mass marketed paperback in the grass next to the lounge chair. The slam of a back door as kids that seem to belong to no one run in and out, in and out. Back to School Sale flyers littered on front porches. The mercury that continues to climb on the gas station thermometer. The heatwave threat in the 10-day forecast. The warm water coming out of the garden hose. The gnat and its insistence on flying inches from your face. The glass of iced tea, cold and, like most things we think we might love, enticing, but far too sweet and cloying to the taste.

SPOILED

On the night that my brother was born in cold November, my mother picked herself up from the kitchen floor where she'd been scrubbing the linoleum like her life depended on it, and figured that maybe the backache she'd had all day might be labor. Later at the hospital she felt afraid in her pink chenille robe, while my father drank Sanka out of a cardboard cup, while watching Seventy Seven Sunset Strip in the waiting room. On the night that I was born, my mother was so desperate to deliver she began to read the sweat on her palms like tea leaves. As I cascaded down the birth canal, a nurse shrieked for her to close her legs as the doctor, a stodgy man with a limp, had not yet arrived. Out of nerves or boredom , one nurse left the room for a cigarette, and another kept watch for the doctor in the hallway. I came despite all measures to prevent it, imprinted indelibly and forever with urgency and impatience. The doctor scolded my mother for not waiting. My mother would forever despise the month of January. Because the folly of two was not enough my parents left the house early one morning in May as the contractions were coming hard and fast. I had been curled in the warm crook of my mother's knees and cried when I woke and she wasn't there. I remember holding my brother's hand at my Aunt's house. My brother wore a cowboy hat and had a face full of expectation. On the phone my mother sounded happier than I'd ever heard , and her voice was uncharacteristically soft and sounded so far away. She asked us to name the baby, so we did. I remember crying for no good reason that I could ever discern. I tried to pronounce the name in my small mouth , but couldn't pronounce the last vowel. It didn't matter. Everyone called her *love bug* anyway.

ATTENDING MASS WITH MY 90 YEAR OLD FATHER

We genuflect and then slide into the last pew. My father reminds me, as he does each week, that he cannot kneel. I nod. He sits and leans back, crosses his legs at the ankles and folds his hands in his lap. Leavened each week is his belief that every day might be his last chance. It bakes and rises. It is nurtured with furtive prayers. This much I know. Every word he attempts to confide in me comes during the hour in that pew each week. I wait for him to unlock a mystery I have been wanting to know for my entire life. But everytime he opens his mouth, what follows is a series of false starts. He is the patron saint of duty. He will show up as long as he has breath. God reads his mind and reads his heart, but I can know only what he will tell me. When he rises to receive communion, I walk behind him as he heads toward the altar unsteadily, and with great effort. He holds out his large and gnarled hands to receive his Sunday bread. Afterwards, he tells me that he sees so many people he doesn't know. *Why is that?* he asks. He adds that he couldn't hear a single word that the priest had said. *Or didn't say.*

CHRONOTYPE

Loneliness was nurtured on Sundays. Shuttered windows, early supper. I'd dig through drawers of junk , initiating a lifelong obsession with discovery, of something, anything. My mother sleeping on the couch with an afghan of her own making was a touchstone of childhood. Her Benson & Hedges waiting to be lit. She'd say *Wake me up in five minutes* and my heart took a journey all on its own. Five minutes would turn into hours. I cannot locate my sister in my memory, almost as if my own loneliness wrapped me in its scratchy shroud and shut out the world. I did not seek others to alleviate long stretches of time that seemed endless. I watched the kitchen clock, my mother's Timex watch, I called TIME on the telephone to hear the voice of someone who would tell me something. I waited longer intervals to wake my mother so that there would be little resistance when I gave a vigorous shake of her arm. I lifted her lids. I blew my sticky breath into her face. On the television Sea Hunt with Lloyd Bridges in his subterranean world filled the room with blue light and an underwater heartbeat. I couldn't locate my father or my brother. Even the family dog had gone off into a world of its own. I curled into the overstuffed chair facing my mother. I willed time to stand still so that everyone of us could catch up with one another. We'd be happy to be outside of the house, facing a bright and burning sun. We would be outside of the limits of time and hours and hours and hours and hours away from sleep.

MANIFOLD ILLUSIONS WE MISTAKE FOR HAPPINESS

are not at all like dreams. It's the spilt sugar on the Formica countertops, the tongue that flicks the grains that make the teeth shudder like the tremor of premature death. It's mistaking the milk for the honey. It is the look of astonishment for one of lust. The noise the change in the pocket makes for wealth. It's staying in the chase without love. It is the stare without being seen. It is the touch without being warmed, or transformed. It's the road ahead but without a single place to go. It is the place but no space for you when you get there. It's the intense desire without the available opportunity. It's the chance without the sparkling wheel to spin. It's the warm cup overflowing but still feeling parchedness. It's that vertiginous feeling without cause. It's whatever is sweet in the moment, whatever we need to carry on. It's bitter after taste. The manifold illusions we mistake for happiness are not at all like dreams. *But they might as well be.*

VIA VECCHIA

I keep my distance from the old widow in black polyester and wool, a string bag hanging on her arm. She squints at the sun with milky eyes. She is an old spell caster. Her children were never born though they remain bloated and moaning , within her. One red thread runs through her black, gathered skirt. She is the embodiment of unspoken and unfulfilled desires come to roost. The ancient cobble stone retains a heat that rises through my feet , but I am grateful that my legs can still take me where I want to go. I move from her line of sight. On *Via Vecchia* , the vacant eyes of the pleasure seekers are glazed with a wanton desire that frightens me. The sea pulls them forth with its own incantations. I have been the victim of intensity masked as good intentions. In a way, I, too, am a widow, staking a claim to something already gone that gives me my persistent identity, something lost along the narrow way. *Misfortune is catching.* Proximity to it is the danger we entertain unaware, while sipping our milky coffee out of rimless cups and picking at our meals. The rind of lemon curls in the sun and we smell its fragrance everywhere. The evening is a menace that stays up late. I see the outline of the widow through her threadbare curtain and it awakens a latent memory in me that is best forgotten. She lights a candle, and her blue veined hands hover over the small flame. I am buffeted by revulsion and desire for a life that is anywhere, anywhere but here. The decay is palpable. I can hear drunken revelers far from home. I see children eating gelato, and young lovers smoking in the desultory ways that only they can. The rumble of the sea is no match for its extreme blue under a sky that we can still count on. Someone breaks a glass. The candle is extinguished. At night, the sky we thought we knew is devoid of stars , but I gave up reading signs long ago. My mother with her inherited superstition warned me to never let the dead kiss me in a dream and yet, I purse my lips when opportunity presents itself. I stumble, for sure, but I still find my way home, kissed by salt air, guided by a generational imperative as native to me as the bright yellow lemons abundant and tart.

ANOINTED

There is a kind of indifference that is bespoke, made just for you. The reddest of flags flap and wave while something sinister, but oh so exciting happens in the background . We often confuse the two. The bluest moon is also said to be the coldest, and I should know since I have shuddered in its shadow. I've stopped verifying sources, and I've lost track of so many things. Give us this day our daily milk, and let everyone else preach a deficit narrative to live by. The stone in my pocket is both amulet and burden. I walk with my hands clasped behind my back like a little old man who thinks he still has a place to go. I follow in the footsteps of shiny crows who are forlorn, and thirsty. There is a society of late bloomers on the edge of a precipice who only need a reason. A weather change is considered redemptive to most , but you must be prepared for it. A change of scenery means a change of heart. I could be a blue crab scuttling across a black beach. I could be in a city I pronounce in a foreign accent with a flair as I lean against a tall cypress that has surely appeared in a painting by a famous artist. I wait because I am said to be patient that way. Everything in time. *Eventually, hard rain. Strong wind. Bright candles.*

SOMEWHERE IN CALABRIA, 1952

There are internal monologues one might practice riding alone on a train. Broad patterns of history reveal themselves just on the other side of thick glass windows. An American soldier sits with his cold feet in thick boots. Is this peacetime or might this be a different kind of a war? He presses his fingers together. It looks like prayer, but really, he is only trying to link his phobias to the trauma unseen. He sees tiny altars of blackened and broken statues of saints in his waking dreams. He is far from his mother who at that exact moment leans over the kitchen sink. Her patron saint has turned his back on her and her heart keeps going to the place where she misses her son. He can hear the hollow of his father's accented silence, filling the hollows of space within him. Give us this day our daily bread, a crust left in his pocket, an orange placed into his hands by his mother's aunt. He is the first American she has ever seen and thinks he is so tall, he can conquer the world. He peels the orange, and sees rows of hyssop through the window on the dry grass as they pass by, which makes him long for anointing. The smell of the orange reached some on the train, who disliked the American and his uniform on sight. His long Roman nose and his thick black hair hold no currency. Their smiles have forgotten joy, so inconveniently he gets off at the next stop. The orange rind curls in on itself on the grimy floor, under the cracked leather seat that is still warm, leaving a trace of him despite his departure.

AT THE ROOT

The teeth in the jar took on a life of their own. Like a disembodied jaw with something important to say, but stubbornly silent. His and hers glasses, half full, one jaw larger than the other placed right next to the votive candle near the Sacred Heart, framed in faded and splintered wood, a relic from the old country. I dipped my fingers one by one into the wax, just beneath that dancing flame and felt the heat like an illicit kiss. I stared into the heart with thorns that pierced, and felt pain that I thought was real. My grandparents looked old and poor without their teeth, and their teeth looked lonely in their watery resting place. There were never enough occasions for them to wear them. They'd both had teeth in their heads extracted on the same day. The Scandinavian dentist with the pipe plucked them one by one as if kernels off an ear of rotting corn. He dropped them into a metal bowl for effect. *Clink, clink, clink.* He was amused by such a request and thought of them as the *dagos* he believed them to be, and too lazy to take care of their own teeth, on top of everything else that rubbed him the wrong way. My grandmother aged overnight but her newly puckered mouth looked happier than it usually did. Their relationship to their new teeth was tenuous; teeth were one more sorrow on an otherwise crowded and full plate. Still, my grandmother would carefully brush both sets of dentures. It was rare, but when she wore them, she'd stiffen her back, and pray her novena's in a language that seemed altogether new to her, syllables catching behind an artificial gumline and sticking to the roof of her mouth. I decoded the *click, click, click* of certain words, weaving a narrative to suit my own purposes. As for me, I tongued my way through my own decayed and missing teeth, lingering in the empty spots filled with a seeds of sorrow I would never, for the life of me, be able to name.

PORTRAIT OF GREAT-GREAT GRANDPARENTS

The unmistakable look of fear in their eyes is what one notices first. Their bodies are positioned as though they do not know what to do with themselves or their arms, their heads, or what might be expected of them, unlettered, brutally practical, desires universally unspoken. Her thin and graying hair is parted severely down the middle, braided and wound around the top of her head like a crown. Small gold earrings, the only jewelry she owned, adorn her large earlobes. Her breasts, surely once ample and a point of pride, sag to her thick waist, dejected, no longer of any practical use. Her husband's face looks as though it is about to issue a warning or a threat, and covered in short, white whiskers. His coat is worn, his pants faded and thin. They stand together against a painted bucolic scene as a backdrop that belies the poverty, deprivation, and the peculiar pagan tendencies intertwined with sanctioned incantations that marked their long days. One imagines the reason for the photograph to be something official, but it would be difficult to imagine what that might be. We cannot see their love, their scars, cannot intuit their emotions, or how they negotiated the brutal existence they were born into. The piercing eyes are communicating something lost to posterity. After the photograph was taken, I imagine they shuffled off and out of the makeshift studio. I imagine that he might be the first to leave through the heavy wooden door, squinting up at the sun and doffing his heavy coat. No doubt, she follows behind him slowly at first, then quickening her pace as best as she can, trying to catch up with the man she has been yoked to since she was practically a girl in long silky braids, majestic on her wedding day, though. Always and forever behind, and trying to catch up.

SCHEMATIC

Death is a numbers game. *It comes in threes, my mother* says. Sorrow disorients. *What time of the day is it anyway*, my mother asks, though the large clock on the wall ticks. We stand at the casket and observe a thin man in gray slacks, burgundy wool vest. White shirt. His immobile arms by this side. He wears his eyeglasses in death as he did in life. *They did a good job with him*, my mother declares, but only I can see the shudder of her small, rounded shoulders. Small details come into view with great purpose. The slight scar over the left eye, and the right hand turned inward. My mother's sister stands so small next to the casket of her husband. *I still can't believe he's gone.* Somewhere a luncheon is being prepared, butter for rolls , soup with canned vegetables mixed in and plenty of coffee for the grieving. I have forgotten the sound of his voice, so I pretend it was not full of sarcasm and sorrow. A priest is stringing words together for a man he has never met in life. A child stealthily inches out of the pew and gives the pall a tug. I cannot speak or move. My eyes would tell a story if someone looked into them. It slides off the casket and onto the polished ecclesiastical squares of the church floor. *Lift up your hearts*, the priest intones. The pall is in a heap. The casket is left momentarily bare and exposed, the gleam of the gold plated cross atop of it, gleaming. An omen as clear as any for those who are inclined to interpret things that way.

SUNDAY SINATRA

While my mother diced onion and crushed plum tomatoes with her hands, my brother would take the Sinatra album out of its cardboard cover, careful to handle it on the sides as we were taught. He would place it on the turntable and tape a penny to the arm of the needle and lightly let it drop. Every Sunday was Sunday Sinatra, and as my father would galavant around town, she started the gravy on the stove, fried the meatballs and poured the remaining oil into the pot. We waited every Sunday for the midday meal like it was a holiday. The water for macaroni wouldn't boil until my mother laid down her apron, and replaced Sinatra with , with the Pennsylvania Polka album. My mother rearranged the thick black curls on the back of her head, and activated her third eye, telling us for the thousandth time how my father hated polka. *He should be here any minute,* she'd say, with a laugh. Sure as anything, he'd come through the door, wiping his feet and stepping over the threshold. My brother changed the record as if on command. My mother, playful to my father's serious nature, would drape her arm across his shoulders and take his other hand in hers and they would lightly dance in a circle until their feet would rise right off the braided rug and they were floating together, above us. Sinatra crooned in our living room and in the kitchen warm with steam. I would open the navy blue box of Conte Luna pasta. It was rigatoni, my father's favorite. My brother raised the blue flame under the pot and brought the water to a rapid boil.

PINNED

The accumulation of safety pins on my blouse was not a feat of animal mastery, like the dressage I was always so fascinated by. The trained , well muscled body of a horse with muscle memory performing on a barely discernible command. The beauty of it stunned me. The pins were a simple accumulation of superstition and disappointment, a reminder of my various entrapments and inevitable fallibility. I wore that blouse until it was threadbare, when the pins barely clung to the silky , dejected threads. There was no purpose anymore. I'd collected the pins for *just in case* scenarios, as if doing so was a solution for every problem I might encounter. I'd fiddle with the clasp. Open close, open close. Pierced my thumb, once, twice, three times. Felt the bloom of blood like an imagined scenario in a faraway place, and not like the last attempt gesture it might really have been. The tail of the shirt bloomed beautiful small red flowers , a testament to the kind of garden that a peculiar and carefully curated anxiety tends to grow.

SACCHARINE

At the coarse grained table a man with three days stubble stares into the jade green cup at the dark coffee within. Here is a man who skips Novocain for a cavity, and takes his showers ice cold and bracing, but the black coffee that smells nearly medicinal to him. He has such a longing for sweetness these days and will get it where he can. When his wife shuffles into the kitchen, he is meticulously dropping brown sugar crystals, one by one into the liquid abyss. This takes some precision not to mention patience on his part. She watches as he lightly rolls each crystal between thumb and forefinger before letting it go. This could take some time to get the desired flavor. She thinks he surely must realize this. She decides not to speak this time, but she can't suppress the ridiculousness of the scene. She takes her own coffee out on the patio where she considers lighting a cigarette, craving the strong bitter flavor on her tongue. She feels the thick hand on the back of her neck and hears the back door slam. Or maybe it is the other way around. She isn't sure. She knows that the tree stump near the flagstone of the patio is soon speckled with her blood. She will have to wash her hair. This annoys her. She apologetically tells the officer that neither of them can help themselves, but she has no idea why. *"Listen,"* she holds up her finger for emphasis, *"I'm not going to sugar coat it anymore."* The officer nods, looking at her husband already in handcuffs. He shrugs. Her statement strikes a false note. The officer takes the husband in his cruiser to the station. Half pities him. Breaks the rules by stopping for coffee first. The husband leans forward in the back seat, hands cuffed behind his back. *"Large. Black. No Sugar."*

BOTH SIDES NOW

Closed street market at sunset in Sicily. The cats prowl the littered gutters. I step over fish bones, rotten fruit and a wine bottle still plugged with its cork, laying on its side in sorrow as if it had been left at the altar. The expansiveness of the market is the opposite of niche. The assault of smells reminds me that I am a body still capable of discernment. Not one hour ago, merchants manned the tables now folded for another day imploring me to part with my money. When I aim my camera at a veritable pyramid of red tomatoes I am shouted at: *Not for looking, for eating!* And though the scene is commonplace to me there are things I am in fear of forgetting. There is an imperative to get the details straight. There are stories I want to tell, and the photographs would provide proof: *I was here, I exist.* A man on the corner smokes a cigarette and watches me as I walk down the center of the market like a runway. *Or so I think.* He turns from me and blows smoke up to the sky. The nicotine hangs in the humid air, heavy and dank. I am nothing among the vast amount of things there are to offer. A group of boys kicks a soccer ball back and forth, as the glow of the sun recedes. I look for a familiar face to pass the time with, but am left with myself. The graffiti that covers the walls everywhere contains messages I decode and take to heart. *Salvatore ama Mariella* is scrawled with abandon in large loopy letters, and I feel something stir. Loneliness is an empty nave, a friendship in flux, a broken key left in a lock that no longer will open. Further down at the end of the market, I see one apple left in a broken crate, bruised on one side, but shiny and rounded, delicious, and desperately desired on the other.

MY MOTHER SINGS SO THAT MY FATHER CAN SLEEP

In casual conversation // my mother lets it slip //that she sings my father to sleep.// My father looks down //with a smile on his face// then crosses his arms across his chest.// *Don't I?* My mother asks my father// who would never contradict her.// My mother cannot sing// though she has done quite a bit of it in her lifetime.// As a child I remember how she loved to sing //mocking little ditties on every occasion. // It made my face bloom with shame.// Her transistor radio moved from kitchen// to bathroom// and down to the cellar // where she did our laundry. //My father, a light sleeper and // quasi insomniac now listens to her songs// as his head lies on the pillow they sometimes share// beside her, warm under many layers of blankets.// They've walked the road so long together now// it is twilight, and they recede in almost imperceptible ways to the rest of us //but it all makes sense to them.// Her breath in my father's ear//my mother sings my father to sleep// and just like that// he closes his eyes.

EMMA MORANO DIED AT 117 YEARS OF AGE

Garlanded in her rosary beads and polyester house dress, she kept things simple. This "sculptural simplicity" as her parish priest liked to say, was out of step with the times, both then and now. In a one pot kitchen she cooked for herself, and delighted in her solitude crediting longevity to the lack of a husband. One can relate to Emma in Verbania, Italy. She would not suffer the indignities that a husband would surely impose, and grieved the loss of a son who she knew she would see, one day, in perfect form. It was all so long ago. Three raw eggs in a glass and down the gullet every day was a ritual. Collector of clocks, quiet passer of time, *tick, tick, tick.* Visitors always stayed too long. She would pull the red and blue stripe knitted vest over her head to keep away the chill. A resignation undefined would pass through her body, like a beckoning. *Touch the blind. Caress the cheek of a baby.* Everybody wants to know the secret. The price of fame. *Show us how to live.* How to bow our heads first thing in the morning and the last thing at night. People pray to her as though she were a saint. Emma, what can we say, but that we are all so *enormously* grateful.

LATE MARRIAGE

If love strikes you dumb, blame yourself. It's not an IQ test, but maybe it should be. Swept off your feet after a certain age can feel as though in constant and exhilarating flight. You embrace a new self, your pupils dilate , and you just want to be a better person. The object of your affection is marriage-minded. How rare! Lost chances are still chances whose luck has changed. Diamonds are forever and at your age, your late marriage would be, too. The distance from you and the grave has shortened. Your sense of time encroaches, increasing urgency. Yes, a late marriage would be lovely. An understated dress. A bridegroom in navy blue. The celebrant someone who is mail order certified would suffice and make everything easier. A party not a reception. *We won't live forever* is your battle cry. But then, the coffee mug in the sink. The dragging of slippered feet across the carpet. The dog who strains his bowels in the backyard. The six inches of water in the basement after the rain. The calls that go unanswered. The red flags that become banners in your peripheral vision. The dress under thick plastic , yellows. The diamond digs a hole into the delicate skin of your finger. Your bridegroom says *what's the rush* out of nowhere. Late marriage when it happens, if it happens, is late. *It's just too late.* A wingless bird sings a paean to what is yet to come. Give him his due. Pay attention. *Live to see the day.*

DEAD LETTER

One January a friend was buried. As my fingertips burned with bitter cold, I thought warmth forever an impossibility. My friend loved the sun and had a perpetual tan, even in winter. I'd seen him turn his face to the sky so many times, closing his eyes to some private reverie where he transcended himself. In summer, his iced tea, cigarettes and lawn chair were satisfying to him in a way I thought paltry; I blamed him for always playing it small. I was ignorant of his inner life. His simplicity angered me. He spoke of Florida , a place he'd visited as a child, like a mythical place, unattainable to him. When I stabbed my finger on a map to show him how close we were, that his "dream" could be fulfilled with ease—not that far—-I couldn't have known his barriers were not mere miles. Before they lowered him into the ground, I placed a handful of dirt on his coffin, a custom I was unacquainted with. I apologized to him for the frozen ground, the iron gray sky, the cold so biting that the Rabbi shook and stuttered. I wish him a good journey and a peaceful afterlife, though I knew it was nothing he believed in. If it had to be nothingness, then let it be nothingness. He used to say that January was the worst—an entire month of Mondays. A dead letter that was destined, from the beginning, to never arrive.

A SINGLE SURGE

This year my sorrow is intent on drowning itself. As for me, I can't be responsible for my own ambition anymore. Nail my hair to the floorboards, and watch me lay fallow, my breath slowed to the imperceptible rise of my chest. I am a dying animal, the small kind, all annoyance and inconvenience. Break the brittle, fragile bone in my neck and thumb my dowagers hump in the wayward belief that it might bring you luck. Disfigurements are all the rage, but they don't work as hard as they used to. The childless women and the women whose bodies are excoriated for giving their unborn a place to live have more in common than they think they do. Blood and membrane provide the scaffold. Let society have their say. Our mouths still move long after our bodies have said *enough*. Words are brandished like a whip that I snap just to hear the sound of it. I used to be able to circle my waist with my arms, but no more. There is an ache to nothingness and that, in and of itself is ironic. I am displaced in a familiar setting, denying the gloss , that particular shine this is mine. At the ancestral level, let me say I am grateful for inheritance. At the collective level, I have something to offer: whispered remedies and unguents to ease the burn. Everyone waits for me. *This temple. These peonies. These poets who scratch earnestly in their notebooks, self-glorifying so that we believe the hype. The transformation of all the fables I have told myself.* And still, I cannot, without distortion, make my highly articulate prayers heard beyond the chambers of my own barbed wire heart.

AGAINST A PRESCRIPTIVE LEGACY

It was all going to be a story anyway, and I always wanted to tell it with a flair. My father checked off the *do's* and *should's* he kept in an imaginary ledger by the side of his bed. My mother crumpled hers in her house dress pocket with her tissues and her yellow box of Chiclets. I watched from different vantage points, and tried to fit where I wasn't wanted and eschewed all of the places where I was. A therapist once told me that it appeared that I was confused by many things, a confusion born of a trauma, indeed, an early trauma. She was so sure of it. I just settled into ambiguity, uncertainty, chance. It was all laid out for me, but I couldn't have found my way with a guide. I had to leave the country a half dozen times before I could refer to myself as *me*. Who was I without the expectation of belonging or the legacy of my grandmother's stoic patience in the face of unearned cruelty? I lay my well-thumbed cards on the table. I choose carefully. I paid attention to the phases of the moon, the waxing and waning experienced by all of us if we pay attention, but only felt with acuity by those who need both its atmosphere and exosphere. Bottle the apprehension in a clouded jar by the door. Adjust the decorative gas mask to fit the contours of your dumb struck expression, your ridiculous face. A politician we love to hate promises chaos in Biblical proportions. The way is paved and it is not a golden opportunity. This time, above all other times, you must do the opposite of whatever it was you were told, before the before.

CORIUM, 1973

The soft crinkles in my grandmother's skin are a memory I place on the edge of where everything begins. The train cars chugged slowly that Saturday across the tracks and I was so unsentimental about everything. Time was a band I could stretch into infinity. It felt meaningless. In the car, with my mother gripping the steering wheel on a day that felt like it might never end, my grandmother kept her large pocketbook on her lap, with one arm stretched across the back of the old Chevrolet. Her skin looked papery, and I brushed the tips of my fingers across the tips of hers. She never looked back at me, sweating in the back seat thirsty beyond anything I'd ever felt. Back at our house she needed to be persuaded to play hymns on my tabletop organ that wheezed and hummed. She played Rock *of Ages* over and over again with her eyes closed, and then just one *Ave Maria*. Early the next day, she put the coffee pot on the stove, placed her false teeth in her mouth, and sat in the chair by the front window to say her rosary. When she was buried three days later, I thought of what would become of her soft, powdery, and papery skin. My grandfather told us she said goodbye to him before she left, a detail that set our teeth on edge not because it couldn't be true, but because it probably was. He said he held her hand, but for the first time ever, it was rough. The scent of the funeral flowers made me nauseous with grief. The priest spoke so slowly as soft petals fell to the floor and that we walked over without thinking. The forced silence of the grieving was a time bomb ticking in my growing brain. I pulled at the skin of my fingers while time stood still with a stubbornness I wanted to bang my head against. I sucked my bloody fingers, a prisoner in a shell of my own skin and not a single person who loved me to pull me out of hiding.

FORESHADOWED

On Sunday evenings, my grandmother drank her coffee right from the saucer and folded her prescription pills in cottage cheese and grape jelly, but still, she winced as they slid down her throat. She'd give me words of wisdom because she'd had a vision that she wouldn't live long. She'd say *Those with big feet are lucky—they get a firm foundation.* I looked at my own feet growing so rapidly , yet still feeling the ground beneath me bottomless. Years later I suffered spasms under my ribcage like thousands of angry butterflies that were like a metaphor for life—something that was supposed to be beautiful, but could corner and sideswipe you at will. Eventually, all of my internal organs were deemed unremarkable by someone who knows much better than I ever could, but it said nothing of my mind, or my fragile emotional lexicon. I channeled my grandmother's predictable approach, but failed miserably in the execution. In imitation, I drank coffee from saucers and stayed awake most nights listening for an owl she'd always said was an omen of nothing good. *Nothing good.* Out of my head and into the world, I heard the targeted insults, though I was too hardened by my own shame to do anything about them. I had a realistic appreciation of most situations and learned a valuable lesson that I will never forget: when someone says they wish you well, you can be sure they mean anything but. Truly, as hard a pill as I have ever had to swallow.

THE SLEEPING BEAUTY OF PALERMO

> ". . . Her eyes are not closed and never have been."
> —Dario Piombino-Mascalli

In her glass covered coffin, Rosalia Lombardo sleeps the sleep of the angels. In the Capuchin catacombs, death masquerades as life. The long gone hang from walls in their Sunday best, mouths agape as if astonished at their own improbable conditions The skin of her paper thin eyelids reveals her still blue eyes, as they catch the afternoon light through the side windows. Witnesses like to say she comes to life, that she moves her eyes, and scans the room, watching those who watch her. We have her father to thank for this specimen of a time we can never know. When pneumonia assailed the delicate lungs of Rosalia, one week before her second birthday, as the Spanish Flu surged, she succumbed like so many. Of her mother, we know nothing, but can imagine the fear and the grief. Of her father, we know he could not live without her countenance and asked an embalmer to preserve her as much and as long as was humanly possible. One part glycerin, one part formalin, zinc sulfate, zinc chloride, and salicylic acid injected into the femoral artery, and the family could visit her every Sunday after lunch and before their own repose in the hot afternoons. It should come as no surprise that the silk ribbon tied on the top of her head, on the day of her death, wilts dejectedly, though her baby face is peaceful. Because natural processes can only be delayed, she has begun to turn a waxy yellow, leading the curators of the catacombs to scramble to preserve further deterioration. Now, once on extravagant display, she lies, alone, in a hermetically sealed tiny coffin, where she is no longer visible to curious and morbid onlookers. It comforts me to know that Rosalia is in her dark enclosure, safe from the spectacle that her father initiated, but is no longer around to see, settled into the peaceful eternal sleep that will, eventually, come to us all.

INSENSATE

If I wanted to make certain proclamations I'd speak them into empty rooms, on cold nights, devoid of all sound. I would quiver for effect. I would generate my own predictions, but would refuse private readings, even if implored to do so. I can claim knowledge of certainties, but they come from the past, not the future, which feels like cheating, but it isn't. If I wanted to give advice, that's another story. Still, it might sound like this: If you have known hardship like a boot on the back of your neck, your solitude will feel like your very own fingers scratching your very own back—dissatisfying. If you have to imagine a space for love, not even a big space, maybe just a small space where emotions might fold up like an envelope and slip under your door, you will practically ensure that those eligible will suit themselves first and then wash their hands of you. No explanations will be forthcoming. A Buddhist will tell you "That's life." If when you move forward a bit it feels a lot like what *afterward* feels like, you have probably rescued yourself one time too many. Sympathetic gestures wear the right clothes, but are fraudulent and you gave up reading minds and murmuring agreement long ago. See this room, devoid of human sound? It is like a vessel that is in perpetual motion. You stand on the deck but cannot tell if what you see or feel is moving away from you or coming closer. Let yourself feel the force of gravitational desolation. The trapped fly knows it well. How it enters a room with such ease, knows it isn't wanted, then exhausts itself to utter death trying to find an exit.

INHERITED

I thought my father was capable of holding back flood waters should they rise. I watched him catch fireflies bright like lightning in his calloused hands. Their tiny bodies calibrated their greenish-yellow glow in our mayonnaise and mustard jars with the tops punctured. I held mine like a lantern while my father watched me from the driveway. I wondered what he was thinking then, and I wonder now. Did he know that I was a *strega* in training, would learn to read signs, decode omens? There are cunning folk in our lineage, I always knew that, carried it like a precious jewel within me, emerald, like the patch of tiny front lawn my father tended in the summer. Thick green and carpet-like, but not to walk on, just for show. Just to keep one tiny thing in life nearly perfect and unspoiled. Beauty anywhere was an artifact kept behind glass for safekeeping. My grandfather once took some plastic beans from a game my brother and I loved to play called "Spill the Beans." He planted a few in a pot and tended the soil with an old fork. Miracles seemed dead, but there was evidence everywhere that people still believed. I have memories that frighten me, but they might have been dreams. I can't be sure anymore. I don't want to predict the future and I don't want to rob anyone of their past. My father will no longer listen to my dreams. He leaves the room, rubbing the back of his neck, hobbling on his diabetic feet—he just never wanted to know and that has not changed. He inherited fear like some inherit a cleft lip: genetic and going way, way back. My mother leans in, listens as well as she can, her hearing aids whistling. It is good to note that the beans from the game that my grandfather planted grew thick and strong, beyond anyone's imagination. I have a photo of him with that plant. He holds his dog close by one side, with the large plant all thick roots standing like a sentry on his other side, at least 6 feet tall. I had dreamed of something overtaking us all, when I was only five years old. My father called it a miracle.

UMBRA

On a cold day in June I rocked my granddaughter to sleep. I buried my face in her curls then felt an intense swirl of heat surrounding me. *It rested in my throat.* This came on the heels of a week of ultramarine dreams, which made me feel out of time. I kept pressing my feet into the floor, trying to ground myself. I emptied out a folder of old photos. I focused on one of showing my father in Rome's Piazza del Popolo, his hands deep into the pockets of an overcoat with broad shoulders. Common nightingales in various states of flight surrounded him. He looked pensive, much the way his own father tended to look in photos. *Always an edge of fear.* The colors in the photo were muted with time, much like my father's memory of that day. The sky was such a pale blue, it looked nearly bereft. It awakened a homesickness in me that had thus far been muted. I tracked the cause of past suffering to indecision and maybe a lack of touch. Emotional investments made me realize that I was made for freedom, but the road was narrow. I must have an ancestor somewhere, whose name, long forgotten, meant something important that could be useful to me who could help me to survive certain brutalities. The future may make us tremble, but we will walk into it anyway. Once someone loved me and gave me a diamond ring like my very own star, brilliant, but prone to fading over millennia. Love was a miracle in the way that hysteria is: it comes out of nowhere and no one can make sense of it in time enough for it to matter. There is a photograph of me, but it is a creation of my own imagination. I am wearing a light violet dress. The sun is weak. I am pensive, like my father. I am off to the side, leaving most of the photograph empty. But I have a memory and I want to pass it on to the little one in my arms: behind enormous light, there was a raw purple moon. My blood diamond. A far off summer symphony. Now my ring finger is empty save for the scar where it used to sit like a shining star.

LET NOTHING YOU DISMAY

My father's geographical tendencies were nurtured when he began to walk. His gentle mother's hands on his small shoulders moved him toward or away from things like a guiding light. There was a velocity to his knowing where his feet were planted, fast and fastidious, as if nothing else mattered. The familiarity of blood meant turbulence in the strictest sense of the word, and gave usable information years and years later. Intercessory prayer had us both kneeling at the altar in a church filled to the brim with a visual coding that was second nature to us. The cynical among us called it sorcery, or worse. I had eyes like glass which magnified what I held in the stillborn heart I was born with. I dictated to my father everything I saw. When a murder of crows softly cooed in my general vicinity, I thought of how transitory comfort is to all living things. Here one day, gone the next. My father stood back, crossed his arms in front of him and I knew he feared it was an omen because geography aside, we were a superstitious people, given to signs and symbols, and robed in the inflected dialect we held so close , despite the years. When my father turned from me I pushed away the urge to guide him. We can read each other like a book, but it doesn't mean we have to.. Answers to prayers are eventually bestowed. We hold patience, above all, in pockets where we will dip our hands for reassurance. All in good time. *All in good time.*

ALL THE STARS ARE SHINING

The desires of my heart would require miracles. I spoke this aloud once, among the detritus of the Sunday dinner. The crumpled paper napkins, the sweating glasses of water as though shedding tears. The leftover lettuce wilted in a puddle of wine vinegar. The onions pushed to the side. My father, tired and leaning on his bruised arms, raised his eyes to mine. My mother lifted her eyebrows into her hairline, always the skeptic and unsentimental as they come. Neither of them heard me. I press my feet into the hardwood floor to remind myself of where I am in place and time. I am far from the underground grotto in the land of my ancestors, where I prayed hastily to a forlorn Madonna, not looking heavenward, but instead down at her own feet. I need to tell someone what I felt there, but the bend of my father's back and the hunch of his now bony shoulders has put my concerns on the back burner, telling a story of its own. I can still see the long extinguished candle in a rusted and corroded receptacle at the Virgin's feet. I told them someone surely made a fervent prayer at her feet. My mother says *maybe,* then , *what's for dessert?* I pull the wrong kind of knife through the cold, sugarless blueberry pie as I tell them about a blue room discovered in the ruins of Pompeii, undiscovered for 2,000 years. Ritual activities happened in that room, sacred objects stored there, I tell them, more excited than I feel. *Like a church* my mother says. It is not a question. I envy the surety of their years. The desires mostly put to rest, while mine pulse and throb unanswered. In the grotto, cigarettes were put out at the feet of the sad statue. I remember emerging into darkness so bright, I thought I could see stars in the sky. *And then my eyes adjusted.* My parents slowly get up from the table, settle themselves into their respective chairs facing the television. I put the coffee on. My desires are put on hold. It is what they expect. All part of the ritual, and almost holy in and of itself.

Acknowledgments

I am endlessly grateful to the editors of the following journals in which some of the poems in this collection first appeared, some in slightly different format:

"Sanguination," *Italian-Americana.*
"The Gate Through Which I Entered," *Pikers Press.*
"Somewhere They Worship Fruit," *Roi Faineant.*
"Somnolent," *Bending Genres.*
"Reliability," "Umbra," *Red Eft.*
"Moot," *A Thin Slice of Anxiety.*
"My Father's X-Ray," & "When Summer Begins to Die," *Lothlorien Poetry Journal*
"If You Should Find Yourself Voiceless," & "At the Core," *New World Writing.*
"Catalytic" and "Volpe," *World City Lit.*
"Canonical," *Uppagus.*
"Superlatives," *Literary Heist*
"Modigliani Knew Them All," *Ekphrastic Review.*
"Suburban Neighborhood Pastoral," "Solleone," &"When Summer Begins to Die," *Literary Yard*
"Truncated," *Quail Bell Magazine*
"Fever Dream," *Thimble Literary Magazine*
"Attending Mass With My 90 Year Old Father," *Afterpast Review*
"Via Vecchia," *Mediterranean Odyssey*
"Mussolini's Balcony," "Elemental" *Setu Bilingual Journal*
"At the Root," Atrium Poetry
"The Old Country," *Shelia na Gig*
"Manifold," *Third Street Review*
"Elemental," *Tipton Poetry Review*
"Let it be Extravagant," "Misinterpreted," *-ette Review*

"Atavistic," "Both Sides Now," "My Mother Sings," and "Emma Morano Dies at 117 Years of Age," *Mackinaw Review*
"Insensate," *One Art Literary Journal*
"Late Marriage," and "A Single Surge," *Eunoia Review*
"The Sleeping Beauty of Palermo," *Spillwords*
"Let Nothing You Dismay," *Synchronized Chaos*.

About the Author

MICHELLE REALE is the author of several poetry and flash collections, including *Season of Subtraction* (Bordighera Press, 2019) and *Blood Memory* (Idea Press), and *In the Year of Hurricane Agnes* (Alien Buddha Press). She is the Founding and Managing Editor for both OVUNQUE SIAMO: New Italian-American Writing and The Red Fern Review. She teaches poetry in the MFA program at Arcadia University.

VIA Folios

A refereed book series dedicated to the culture of Italians and Italian Americans.

DANIELA GIOSEFFI. *Stardust Lives in Us*. Vol. 186. Poetry.
CARLA PANCIERA. *One Trail of Longing, Another of String*. Vol. 185. Poetry.
LIBBY CATALDI. *It Takes a Lifetime to Learn How to Live*. Vol. 184. Memoir.
DANIELLE JONES. Hunger. Vol. 183. Poetry.
GIOSE RIMANELLI. *Benedetta in Guysterland*. Vol. 182. Literature.
DANTE DI STEFANO. *The Widowing Radiance*. Vol. 181. Poetry.
ANNA MONARDO. *The Courtyard of Dreams*. Vol. 180. Novel.
MATTHEW CARIELLO. *Colloquy of Mad Tom*. Vol. 179. Poetry.
GRACE CAVALIERI. *Fables from Italy and Beyond*. Vol. 178. Poetry.
LAURETTE FOLK. *Eleison*. Vol. 177. Novel.
FRANCES NEVILL. *Coquina Soup*. Vol. 176. Literature.
FRANCINE MASIELLO. *The Tomb of the Divers*. Vol. 175. Novel.
PIETRO DI DONATO. *Collected Stories*. Vol. 174. Literature.
RACHEL GUIDO deVRIES. *The Birthday Years*. Vol. 173. Poetry.
MATTHEW MEDURI. *Collegiate Gothic*. Vol. 172. Novel.
THOMAS RUGGIO. *Finding Dandini*. Vol. 171. Art History.
TAMBURRI GIORDANO GARDAPHÈ. *From the Margin*. Vol. 170. Anthology.
ANNA MONARDO. *After Italy*. Vol. 169. Memoir.
JOEY NICOLETTI. *Extinction Wednesday*. Vol. 168. Poetry.
MARIA FAMÀ. *Trigger*. Vol. 167. Poetry.
WILLI Q MINN. *What? Nothing*. Vol. 166. Poetry.
RICHARD VETERE. *She's Not There*. Vol. 165. Literature.
FRANK GIOIA. *Mercury Man*. Vol. 164. Literature.
LUISA M. GIULIANETTI. *Agrodolce*. Vol. 163. Literature.
ANGELO ZEOLLA. *The Bronx Unbound ovvero i versi bronxesi*. Vol. 162. Poetry.
NICHOLAS A. DiCHARIO. *Giovanni's Tree*. Vol. 161. Literature.
ADELE ANNESI. *What She Takes Away*. Vol. 160. Novel.
ANNIE RACHELE LANZILLOTTO. *Whaddyacall the Wind?*. Vol. 159. Memoir.
JULIA LISELLA. *Our Lively Kingdom*. Vol. 158. Poetry.
MARK CIABATTARI. *When the Mask Slips*. Vol. 157. Novel.
JENNIFER MARTELLI. *The Queen of Queens*. Vol. 156. Poetry.
TONY TADDEI. *The Sons of the Santorelli*. Vol. 155. Literature.
FRANCO RICCI. *Preston Street • Corso Italias*. Vol. 154. History.
MIKE FIORITO. *The Hated Ones*. Vol. 153. Literature.
PATRICIA DUNN. *Last Stop on the 6*. Vol. 152. Novel.
WILLIAM BOELHOWER. *Immigrant Autobiography*. Vol. 151. Literary Criticism.
MARC DIPAOLO. *Fake Italian*. Vol. 150. Literature.
GAIL REITANO. *Italian Love Cake*. Vol. 149. Novel.
VINCENT PANELLA. *Sicilian Dreams*. Vol. 148. Novel.
MARK CIABATTARI. *The Literal Truth: Rizzoli Dreams of Eating the Apple of Earthly Delights*. Vol. 147. Novel.

MARK CIABATTARI. *Dreams of An Imaginary New Yorker Named Rizzoli.* Vol. 146. Novel.
LAURETTE FOLK. *The End of Aphrodite.* Vol. 145. Novel.
ANNA CITRINO. *A Space Between.* Vol. 144. Poetry
MARIA FAMÀ. *The Good for the Good.* Vol. 143. Poetry.
ROSEMARY CAPPELLO. *Wonderful Disaster.* Vol. 142. Poetry.
B. AMORE. *Journeys on the Wheel.* Vol. 141. Poetry.
ALDO PALAZZESCHI. *The Manifestos of Aldo Palazzeschi.* Vol 140. Literature.
ROSS TALARICO. *The Reckoning.* Vol 139. Poetry.
MICHELLE REALE. *Season of Subtraction.* Vol 138. Poetry.
MARISA FRASCA. *Wild Fennel.* Vol 137. Poetry.
RITA ESPOSITO WATSON. *Italian Kisses.* Vol. 136. Memoir.
SARA FRUNER. *Bitter Bites from Sugar Hills.* Vol. 135. Poetry.
KATHY CURTO. *Not for Nothing.* Vol. 134. Memoir.
JENNIFER MARTELLI. *My Tarantella.* Vol. 133. Poetry.
MARIA TERRONE. *At Home in the New World.* Vol. 132. Essays.
GIL FAGIANI. *Missing Madonnas.* Vol. 131. Poetry.
LEWIS TURCO. *The Sonnetarium.* Vol. 130. Poetry.
JOE AMATO. *Samuel Taylor's Hollywood Adventure.* Vol. 129. Novel.
BEA TUSIANI. *Con Amore.* Vol. 128. Memoir.
MARIA GIURA. *What My Father Taught Me.* Vol. 127. Poetry.
STANISLAO PUGLIESE. *A Century of Sinatra.* Vol. 126. Popular Culture.
TONY ARDIZZONE. *The Arab's Ox.* Vol. 125. Novel.
PHYLLIS CAPELLO. *Packs Small Plays Big.* Vol. 124. Literature.
FRED GARDAPHÉ. *Read 'em and Reap.* Vol. 123. Criticism.
JOSEPH A. AMATO. *Diagnostics.* Vol 122. Literature.
DENNIS BARONE. *Second Thoughts.* Vol 121. Poetry.
OLIVIA K. CERRONE. *The Hunger Saint.* Vol 120. Novella.
GARIBLADI M. LAPOLLA. *Miss Rollins in Love.* Vol 119. Novel.
JOSEPH TUSIANI. *A Clarion Call.* Vol. 118. Poetry.
JOSEPH A. AMATO. *My Three Sicilies.* Vol 117. Poetry & Prose.
MARGHERITA COSTA. *Voice of a Virtuosa and Coutesan.* Vol 116. Poetry.
NICOLE SANTALUCIA. *Because I Did Not Die.* Vol. 115. Poetry.
MARK CIABATTARI. *Preludes to History.* Vol 114. Poetry.
HELEN BAROLINI. *Visits.* Vol 113. Novel.
ERNESTO LIVORNI. *The Fathers' America.* Vol 112. Poetry.
MARIO B. MIGNONE. *The Story of My People.* Vol 111. Non-fiction.
GEORGE GUIDA. *The Sleeping Gulf.* Vol 110. Poetry.
JOEY NICOLETTI. *Reverse Graffiti.* Vol 109. Poetry.
GIOSE RIMANELLI. *Il mestiere del furbo.* Vol 108. Criticism.
LEWIS TURCO. *The Hero Enkidu.* Vol 107. Poetry.
AL TACCONELLI. *Perhaps Fly.* Vol. 106. Poetry.
RACHEL GUIDO DEVRIES. *A Woman Unknown in Her Bones.* Vol 105. Poetry.
BERNARD BRUNO. *A Tear and a Tear in My Heart.* Vol. 104. Non-fiction.
FELIX STEFANILE. *Songs of the Sparrow.* Vol. 103. Poetry.
FRANK POLIZZI. *A New Life with Bianca.* Vol. 102. Poetry.

GIL FAGIANI. *Stone Walls.* Vol 101. Poetry.
LOUISE DESALVO. *Casting Off.* Vol 100. Fiction.
MARY JO BONA. *I Stop Waiting for You.* Vol 99. Poetry.
RACHEL GUIDO DEVRIES. *Stati zitt, Josie.* Vol 98. Children's Literature. $8
GRACE CAVALIERI. *The Mandate of Heaven.* Vol 97. Poetry.
MARISA FRASCA. *Via incanto.* Vol 96. Poetry.
DOUGLAS GLADSTONE. *Carving a Niche for Himself.* Vol 95. History.
MARIA TERRONE. *Eye to Eye.* Vol 94. Poetry.
CONSTANCE SANCETTA. *Here in Cerchio.* Vol 93. Local History.
MARIA MAZZIOTTI GILLAN. *Ancestors' Song.* Vol 92. Poetry.
MICHAEL PARENTI. *Waiting for Yesterday: Pages from a Street Kid's Life.* Vol 90. Memoir.
ANNIE LANZILLOTTO. *Schistsong.* Vol 89. Poetry.
EMANUEL DI PASQUALE. *Love Lines.* Vol 88. Poetry.
CAROSONE & LOGIUDICE. *Our Naked Lives.* Vol 87. Essays.
JAMES PERICONI. *Strangers in a Strange Land: A Survey of Italian-Language American Books.*Vol 86. Book History.
DANIELA GIOSEFFI. *Escaping La Vita Della Cucina.* Vol 85. Essays.
MARIA FAMÀ. *Mystics in the Family.* Vol 84. Poetry.
ROSSANA DEL ZIO. *From Bread and Tomatoes to Zuppa di Pesce "Ciambotto".* Vol. 83. Memoir.
LORENZO DELBOCA. *Polentoni.* Vol 82. Italian Studies.
SAMUEL GHELLI. *A Reference Grammar.* Vol 81. Italian Language.
ROSS TALARICO. *Sled Run.* Vol 80. Fiction.
FRED MISURELLA. *Only Sons.* Vol 79. Fiction.
FRANK LENTRICCHIA. *The Portable Lentricchia.* Vol 78. Fiction.
RICHARD VETERE. *The Other Colors in a Snow Storm.* Vol 77. Poetry.
GARIBALDI LAPOLLA. *Fire in the Flesh.* Vol 76 Fiction & Criticism.
GEORGE GUIDA. *The Pope Stories.* Vol 75 Prose.
ROBERT VISCUSI. *Ellis Island.* Vol 74. Poetry.
ELENA GIANINI BELOTTI. *The Bitter Taste of Strangers Bread.* Vol 73. Fiction.
PINO APRILE. *Terroni.* Vol 72. Italian Studies.
EMANUEL DI PASQUALE. *Harvest.* Vol 71. Poetry.
ROBERT ZWEIG. *Return to Naples.* Vol 70. Memoir.
AIROS & CAPPELLI. *Guido.* Vol 69. Italian/American Studies.
FRED GARDAPHÉ. *Moustache Pete is Dead! Long Live Moustache Pete!.* Vol 67. Literature/Oral History.
PAOLO RUFFILLI. *Dark Room/Camera oscura.* Vol 66. Poetry.
HELEN BAROLINI. *Crossing the Alps.* Vol 65. Fiction.
COSMO FERRARA. *Profiles of Italian Americans.* Vol 64. Italian Americana.
GIL FAGIANI. *Chianti in Connecticut.* Vol 63. Poetry.
BASSETTI & D'ACQUINO. *Italic Lessons.* Vol 62. Italian/American Studies.
CAVALIERI & PASCARELLI, Eds. *The Poet's Cookbook.* Vol 61. Poetry/Recipes.
EMANUEL DI PASQUALE. *Siciliana.* Vol 60. Poetry.
NATALIA COSTA, Ed. *Bufalini.* Vol 59. Poetry.
RICHARD VETERE. *Baroque.* Vol 58. Fiction.

LEWIS TURCO. *La Famiglia/The Family*. Vol 57. Memoir.
NICK JAMES MILETI. *The Unscrupulous*. Vol 56. Humanities.
BASSETTI. ACCOLLA. D'AQUINO. *Italici: An Encounter with Piero Bassetti*. Vol 55. Italian Studies.
GIOSE RIMANELLI. *The Three-legged One*. Vol 54. Fiction.
CHARLES KLOPP. *Bele Antiche Stòrie*. Vol 53. Criticism.
JOSEPH RICAPITO. *Second Wave*. Vol 52. Poetry.
GARY MORMINO. *Italians in Florida*. Vol 51. History.
GIANFRANCO ANGELUCCI. *Federico F*. Vol 50. Fiction.
ANTHONY VALERIO. *The Little Sailor*. Vol 49. Memoir.
ROSS TALARICO. *The Reptilian Interludes*. Vol 48. Poetry.
RACHEL GUIDO DE VRIES. *Teeny Tiny Tino's Fishing Story*. Vol 47. Children's Literature.
EMANUEL DI PASQUALE. *Writing Anew*. Vol 46. Poetry.
MARIA FAMÀ. *Looking For Cover*. Vol 45. Poetry.
ANTHONY VALERIO. *Toni Cade Bambara's One Sicilian Night*. Vol 44. Poetry.
EMANUEL CARNEVALI. *Furnished Rooms*. Vol 43. Poetry.
BRENT ADKINS. et al., Ed. *Shifting Borders. Negotiating Places*. Vol 42. Conference.
GEORGE GUIDA. *Low Italian*. Vol 41. Poetry.
GARDAPHÈ, GIORDANO, TAMBURRI. *Introducing Italian Americana*. Vol 40. Italian/American Studies.
DANIELA GIOSEFFI. *Blood Autumn/Autunno di sangue*. Vol 39. Poetry.
FRED MISURELLA. *Lies to Live By*. Vol 38. Stories.
STEVEN BELLUSCIO. *Constructing a Bibliography*. Vol 37. Italian Americana.
ANTHONY JULIAN TAMBURRI, Ed. *Italian Cultural Studies 2002*. Vol 36. Essays.
BEA TUSIANI. *con amore*. Vol 35. Memoir.
FLAVIA BRIZIO-SKOV, Ed. *Reconstructing Societies in the Aftermath of War*. Vol 34. History.
TAMBURRI. et al., Eds. *Italian Cultural Studies 2001*. Vol 33. Essays.
ELIZABETH G. MESSINA, Ed. *In Our Own Voices*. Vol 32. Italian/American Studies.
STANISLAO G. PUGLIESE. *Desperate Inscriptions*. Vol 31. History.
HOSTERT & TAMBURRI, Eds. *Screening Ethnicity*. Vol 30. Italian/American Culture.
G. PARATI & B. LAWTON, Eds. *Italian Cultural Studies*. Vol 29. Essays.
HELEN BAROLINI. *More Italian Hours*. Vol 28. Fiction.
FRANCO NASI, Ed. *Intorno alla Via Emilia*. Vol 27. Culture.
ARTHUR L. CLEMENTS. *The Book of Madness & Love*. Vol 26. Poetry.
JOHN CASEY, et al. *Imagining Humanity*. Vol 25. Interdisciplinary Studies.
ROBERT LIMA. *Sardinia/Sardegna*. Vol 24. Poetry.
DANIELA GIOSEFFI. *Going On*. Vol 23. Poetry.
ROSS TALARICO. *The Journey Home*. Vol 22. Poetry.
EMANUEL DI PASQUALE. *The Silver Lake Love Poems*. Vol 21. Poetry.
JOSEPH TUSIANI. *Ethnicity*. Vol 20. Poetry.

JENNIFER LAGIER. *Second Class Citizen*. Vol 19. Poetry.
FELIX STEFANILE. *The Country of Absence*. Vol 18. Poetry.
PHILIP CANNISTRARO. *Blackshirts*. Vol 17. History.
LUIGI RUSTICHELLI, Ed. *Seminario sul racconto*. Vol 16. Narrative.
LEWIS TURCO. *Shaking the Family Tree*. Vol 15. Memoirs.
LUIGI RUSTICHELLI, Ed. *Seminario sulla drammaturgia*.
  Vol 14. Theater/Essays.
FRED GARDAPHÈ. *Moustache Pete is Dead! Long Live Moustache Pete!*.
  Vol 13. Oral Literature.
JONE GAILLARD CORSI. *Il libretto d'autore. 1860 - 1930*. Vol 12. Criticism.
HELEN BAROLINI. *Chiaroscuro: Essays of Identity*. Vol 11. Essays.
PICARAZZI & FEINSTEIN, Eds. *An African Harlequin in Milan*.
  Vol 10. Theater/Essays.
JOSEPH RICAPITO. *Florentine Streets & Other Poems*. Vol 9. Poetry.
FRED MISURELLA. *Short Time*. Vol 8. Novella.
NED CONDINI. *Quartettsatz*. Vol 7. Poetry.
ANTHONY JULIAN TAMBURRI, Ed. *Fuori: Essays by Italian/American
  Lesbiansand Gays*. Vol 6. Essays.
ANTONIO GRAMSCI. P. Verdicchio. Trans. & Intro. *The Southern Question*.
  Vol 5. Social Criticism.
DANIELA GIOSEFFI. *Word Wounds & Water Flowers*. Vol 4. Poetry. $8
WILEY FEINSTEIN. *Humility's Deceit: Calvino Reading Ariosto Reading Calvino*.
  Vol 3. Criticism.
PAOLO A. GIORDANO, Ed. *Joseph Tusiani: Poet. Translator. Humanist*.
  Vol 2. Criticism.
ROBERT VISCUSI. *Oration Upon the Most Recent Death of Christopher Columbus*.
  Vol 1. Poetry.

www.ingramcontent.com/pod-product-compliance
Lightning Source LLC
Chambersburg PA
CBHW022120090426
42743CB00008B/928